In the Spirit of Wilfred Owen

A New Anthology of Poems

Edited by
Merryn Williams

The Wilfred Owen Association

2002

In the Spirit of Wilfred Owen: A New Anthology of Poems
edited by Merryn Williams

Published by The Wilfred Owen Association, to coincide with the anniversary of the birth of Wilfred Owen, 18 March 1893.
Editor: Merryn Williams
Production: Michael Grayer

© The Wilfred Owen Association, 2002
Copyright of all poems belongs to the authors.
The Wilfred Owen Association would be pleased to hear from those authors whose poems appear anonymously.

ISBN 0-9542302-0-5

Printed by The Chameleon Press
5-25 Burr Road, London SW18 4SQ

Front cover:
Top and middle panels of The Wilfred Owen Window. Installed in Birkenhead Central Library 1995 to commemorate the First World War poet who lived in Birkenhead between 1897 and 1907. Designed by David Hillhouse. Made and installed by William Davis.

Back cover:
Wilfred Owen, newly commissioned Manchester Regiment, 1916.

The Wilfred Owen Association

"My subject is War, and the pity of War.
The Poetry is in the pity …. All a poet can do today is warn"

The Wilfred Owen Association was formed in 1989 to commemorate the life and work of the renowned poet who died in the final week of the First World War.

Philip Larkin described him as "an original and unforgettable poet", "the spokesman of a deep and unaffected compassion".

Owen's poetry retains its relevance and universal appeal; it is certainly much more widely read and appreciated now than at any time since his death, and the Association's international membership represents all backgrounds and levels of scholarship and interest.

Modern scholarship regards Owen's work as the most significant poetry to come out of the 1914-1918 war and his influence on later generations of poets and readers is widely acknowledged.

Since its formation the Association has established permanent public memorials in Shrewsbury and Oswestry. In addition to readings, talks, visits and performances, it promotes and encourages exhibitions and conferences, and awareness of all aspects of Owen's life and poetry.
It publishes regular newsletters.

The Association offers practical support for students of literature and future poets, through links with education, support for literary foundations and information on historical and literary background material.

For membership application or further information, please contact the Chairman:

>Michael Grayer
>Wilfred Owen Association
>c/o 17 Belmont
>>Shrewsbury
>>Shropshire
>>SY1 1TE
>>Great Britain

or visit the Wilfred Owen Association website:

>www.1914-18.co.uk/owen

President:	Peter Owen

Vice-Presidents:	The Earl of Gowrie
	Jill Balcon
	Peter Florence
	Robert Hardy CBE
	Dr Dominic Hibberd
	Professor Jon Stallworthy
	Professor Dennis Welland

Registered Charity Number 702606

Introduction

The idea for this anthology came from a competition back in 1995, for poems 'in the spirit of Wilfred Owen'. Hundreds of poems arrived in Shrewsbury, Wilfred's home-town, and a selection was chosen for publication. This 'spirit' includes many things. Their subject is war, not necessarily the First World War, but they are also a celebration of what he achieved in just twenty-five years.

Wilfred's posthumous life has now lasted three times longer than his real one. Rupert Brooke wrote poems which inspired young men to die bravely; Siegfried Sassoon expressed the anger many people felt at a later stage, and both had a large audience in the years 1914-18. But Owen published very few poems in his lifetime, they were not much noticed, and his reputation took quite a long time to grow. All his readers, even the earliest, knew that he had been killed and this has made a difference to the way they feel about him. Because he himself was a victim, he has the authority to speak for all victims of war.

He became more and more popular as the twentieth century continued on its bloody course and we grew more aware of war, on our television screens if not in person. Today, he has joined the young icons; as Neil Hall writes, he couldn't have been expected to die 'peacefully, in a home for the elderly'. It hardly seems possible to discuss war, particularly the First World War, without quoting him. His phrases have become part of the language; there are novels called *Strange Meeting, Too Few for Drums* and *Blood is Dirt* and a serious historical study called *The Pity of War*. He provided the lyrics for Britten's *War Requiem* and was the inspiration for Pat Barker's best-selling trilogy. He has been portrayed in the film *Regeneration* and several plays. War Art, paintings and drawings have been inspired by his words; he is commemorated by a striking modern sculpture, 'Symmetry', in the grounds of Shrewsbury Abbey; Roger Garfitt's 'Border Songs' are inscribed on glass in Shrewsbury Records Office. He is much loved by fellow-poets and also by the many intelligent ordinary readers who think contemporary poetry is not for them.

It seemed high time to collect the best poems where his spirit is somehow present. Several actually refer to Wilfred Owen but there are others that acknowledge him indirectly. Tony Harrison quotes him when contemplating modern 'squaddies'; so does the late John Ward, remembering a relative executed for desertion. Isobel Thrilling, watching children play with guns in the Museum of Artillery at Woolwich, echoes 'Arms and the Boy'. Others get their inspiration not from poetry but from war itself. Jim Quinn was a soldier in the Gulf and his image of a baby's shoe is reminiscent of Owen's letter in September 1918, 'I kick joyfully about the debris, and only feel a twinge of sadness when a little child's copy-book or frock or crumpled little hat is laid bare'.

The oldest poets in this volume are those who actually witnessed the Great War; Edmund Blunden and two Germans – Peter Baum (1869-1916), killed working as a grave digger on the Western Front, and Gerrit Engelke (1890-1918). The last-named fought in the trenches opposite Owen, died three weeks before him and had so much in common with him that they could easily have had a conversation like the one in 'Strange Meeting'.

The Second World War threw up a new generation of poets who had been influenced by the literature of 1914-1918. Vernon Scannell writes about the long shadow cast by the war he did *not* fight in. Keith Douglas admired Thomas rather than Owen, but obviously could not have written 'Landscape with Figures' if he had not read 'The Show'. Denys L. Jones reworks 'Strange Meeting' in the light of his own experience in 'Cain in the Jungle'. There are the same half-rhymes, the same biblical imagery, the same sense that 'the poetry is in the pity'; even the 'spotted panther' may be a relative of Owen's tigress. The speaker has killed a man of another race, probably Japanese, and bitterly regrets it; the physical and political differences between them ought not to have mattered because both are members of the human family. Unlike the narrator of 'Strange Meeting', this killer is a survivor and there can be no reconciliation between these two men.

There are also younger poets (Ted Hughes, Michael Longley) who are vividly aware of The Great War because they had fathers who fought in it. Hughes' 'Wilfred Owen's Photographs' refers to the legend (it is only that) that Owen kept a set of horrifying pictures to show to people who were complacent about the war. Hughes wrote in 1992 that his idea 'was a true inspiration'. Photographs of that suffering, he believed, would force people to imagine it and therefore to feel it, and do something about it. In fact, what Owen was trying to do was to write a 'photographic representation' of what he had seen, to point out that he had been there and we have not. The politicians in Hughes' poem have no idea of the reality of flogging until they have actually seen the whip.

Today, most people in Western Europe under about sixty have only ever witnessed war on TV. Most poems written from the perspective of a distressed armchair viewer fail dismally. As Owen's biographer Jon Stallworthy reminds us in 'A poem about Poems About Vietnam', those who have not 'been there' cannot write with the authority of those who have. Yet the war lives on, in the loaded revolver of Grevel Lindop's 'The Legacy' and in the 'old, brown, silent film' about Gallipoli, and it is not impossible to write good poetry about it. Theresa Turk, Gladys Mary Coles and the author of 'From a Teashop in Ypres' all consider how, as Owen said, 'the future will forget the dead in war'.

Or you can approach the subject from an unexpected angle. Peter Howard's extraordinary, anarchic poem, 'A Poppy', uses flower images not to prettify but to highlight the craziness of what is happening. Mike Jenkins has Sassoon coming back and behaving badly on VE Day 1995. Judith Kazantzis, writing after the Falklands, questions the whole ethos of patriotism and sacrifice. A lot of women these days are challenging the 'old lie' that war concerns only men.

And then there are the poems that wonder what Owen would have thought of his cult status. There is the paradox that the war which took his life gave him the fame he had long craved. He wasn't just 'the all-time laureate of pain and mud' ('VE Day') but a human being who enjoyed literary pilgrimages (like Victoria Buckley's in 'Scarborough'). Wilfred would have been delighted to be read by children in the twenty-first century ('Legacy') and amused by the idea of being somewhere in Arcadia talking to Keats. I don't think there is anything in this book which would have offended him.

Merryn Williams

Acknowledgements

Grateful acknowledgement is made to the following sources for permission to reproduce poems in this book:

To W.O. and His Kind (Copyright©Edmund Blunden 1940) by Edmund Blunden is reproduced by permission of PFD on behalf of the Estate of Mrs Claire Blunden.

The Act and *The Cycles of Donji Vakuf* by Tony Harrison is reproduced by kind permission of the author.

Wilfred Owen's Photographs by Ted Hughes (from *Lupercal* by Ted Hughes), and *A Picture of Otto* (from *Birthday Letters* by Ted Hughes), reproduced by kind permission of Faber and Faber.

The Legacy Emmer Green 1956 by Grevel Lindop (from Selected Poems by Grevel Lindop) is reproduced by permission of Carcanet Press.

Special thanks are due to David Hillhouse, for permission to reproduce the illustration of the Wilfred Owen Window, and to John Baxter of Birkenhead Central Library.

Contents

ANONYMOUS
In Arcadia — 1
Legacy — 2
V.E. Day — 3
From a Teashop in Ypres — 4
The Lottery — 5
The Dream — 6
Of Poets Dead from War — 7

ROY ASHWELL
Obituaries in the Times for 14th October — 8

PETER BAUM
In 1914 there was a rainbow — 9

EDMUND BLUNDEN
To W.O. and His Kind — 10
To Wilfred Owen — 11

VICTORIA BUCKLEY
Scarborough — 12

IAN CAWS
The Sambre Canal — 13

GLADYS MARY COLES
For the Centenary of Wilfred Owen — 14
N44 France: Holiday Route — 15

MARGARET CRANE
A Drawing Down of Blinds — 16
At the Grave of Wilfred Owen — 17

FRANK DICKINSON
In Memoriam — 18

KEITH DOUGLAS
Landscape with Figures (1) — 19

FREDA DOWNIE
For Wilfred Owen — 20

GERRIT ENGELKE
To the Soldiers of the Great War — 21

ROGER GARFITT
from *Border Songs*
The Haunting — 23

DESMOND GRAHAM
Gloucester — 27

MICHAEL GRAYER
War Without End — 28

JIM GREENHALF
Expression of War Experience — 29

NEIL HALL
Before I get old — 32

TONY HARRISON
The Act (for Michael Longley and James Simmons) — 33
The Cycles of Donji Vakuf — 36

NICK HASLAM
So — 38

PAULINE HAWKESWORTH
The Gas — 39

SEAMUS HEANEY
The Party — 39

NORTON HODGES
At Craiglockhart — 40

GEOFFREY HOLLOWAY
Wilfred Owen — 41

STEPHEN HORSFALL
To Wilfred Owen — 41

PETER HOWARD
A Poppy — 42

TED HUGHES
Wilfred Owen's Photographs — 43

KIT JACKSON
Photograph — 44

JASIM
Identity Card — 45

MIKE JENKINS
Mad Jack Spoils V.E. Day — 46

DENYS L. JONES
Cain in the Jungle — 49

JUDITH KAZANTZIS
For Example Owen — 50

GREVEL LINDOP
The Legacy: Emmer Green 1956   55

KATHLEEN LIVERSIDGE
7 Borage Lane, Ripon   56

MICHAEL LONGLEY
The War Graves   57

BRIAN PATTEN
The Brackets   59

JIM QUINN
The Shoe   60

ALAN RHYS-THOMPSON
Sonnet in Half-Rhyme   61

DAPHNE ROCK
Death Assemblage   62

VERNON SCANNELL
The Great War   64

CHRISTOPHER SOMERVILLE
Saving Owen   65

JON STALLWORTHY
Goodbye to Wilfred Owen   66
A poem about Poems About Vietnam   67

EDWARD STOREY
Red Poppy   68

ISOBEL THRILLING
Museum of Artillery at Woolwich   69

THERESA TURK
Going to Gallipoli   70

WILLIE VERHEGGHE
As a child dying from bullets   71

JOHN WARD
For Private George Ward   72

MERRYN WILLIAMS
Viriconium   73
Wilfred's Bridge   74

***POSTSCRIPT*: TED HUGHES**
A Picture of Otto   76

ANONYMOUS

In Arcadia

Sometimes as I lie awake up here
Breathing the sweetest air
I ponder on what might have been had not
Someone bearing my name been shot
On the Sambre Canal within a week
Of the Armistice.
Sometimes I see myself aged thirty-seven
In 1930, modelling a heaven
Out of more earthly clay, earning a living
At some quotidian trade, having
A wife and child, receiving
From each a caress
As from the sun, the breeze. Sometimes
I dwell upon those other paradigms,
But then I think that ordinariness
Could have destroyed my muse
Or fashioned it to duller fancies, written
In ink rather than blood.
Assuredly what happened was the best
Scenario. The Islands of the Blessed
Are superior to that far scepter'd isle.
Here Keats, my hero, flourishes in style.
We talk on summer nights on the veranda
Exactly as friends should.

Legacy

What is it, within the words of a long-dead soldier
killed at the end of the war (to end all wars)
before the war before the war before this one now,
that moves the children to say
how sorry they feel for the poor bootless
blind deaf tired, choking men
who never came back to Tipperary or to Leicester Square?

Wilfred – what a name! they chortle at first -
was officer material
but his generals used lieutenants
along with the tommies
as green grass to be mown by the scything guns
or silaged in a gas attack.

Something brotherly – quick, boys! – enwraps the classroom,
girls as well, as though a khaki arm
holds each around the shoulder:
each child *can* hear the bitter blood come gargling,
and, with any luck, they won't believe the Lie.

VE Day

Years like the war song's rabbit run.
But I, a Hitler conflict veteran,
Can still remember how our fathers were
Embroiled, embittered in a different war,
Like Wilfred Owen, his genius fulfilled
Then rubbished on the barbed-wire battlefield.
His verse gave voice above the shell and gun,
When hoping ceased and fear unleashed began.
He made death live in lines which crossed an age
To where we mustered at another edge.
This poet of a world on conquest mad,
The all-time laureate of pain and mud,
Was felled, where lesser men fell back,
By guns in stuttering, terminal rebuke.
He left this truth for others to digest,
That war, though sometimes justified, is just
The same old war no one can really win.
We heard. We sighed. We waged another one.

From a Teashop in Ypres

They ordered tea and chose their cakes with care.
Chocolate, deep rich earth-coloured.
Not grey like Flanders mud.

In the coach, the courier had said the visit would be cut short,
'I'm sorry ladies and gents, we have a rushed schedule today
In Ypres.
We have to get back for the visit to the chocolate factory.
Bit unfortunate, but there it is'.

Some left the teashop and found time
To stand at the Menin Gate with the long long list of names.
Then they climbed back into their coach.
For there was more before their date with the chocolate factory.
This was the Tour of the Battlefields
And they would get their money's worth
Of eighty-years-dead men.

In Tyne Cot cemetery there were rows and rows of them.
Tidied away, neat, orderly, a vast filing cabinet
Taming their messy and hideous deaths.
But in Sanctuary Wood they drifted free,
Ghosts, not glimpsed but felt
Among the shrapnel-shot stumps of trees, long dead,
In the pearl-grey melancholy of the November day.

On the journey back, they drove past Passchendaele,
Saw green fields, not the mud that once had choked men's lives away,
Nor their blood and bones, but sheep grazing.
A kind of resurrection?

The chocolate factory was interesting, too.

The Lottery

The war dragged on; our final year at school.
We'd grown too wise for mollifying lies
When some air marshal, ranting on in hall,
Extolled the joys of warring in the skies.
His metal leg too brashly unconcealed,
He talked of wizard shows, he talked of God,
He talked of country, courage in the field:
All missed the mark with this suspicious squad.
The would-be intellectuals, the punks
All sniped at him with insolent advice,
Professing to be pacifists, or funks.
We waited on the throwing of the dice.

The call-up came. We cursed and we obeyed:
No choice, no doubt, we did as we were told.
And some came through unscathed, some maimed, some dead,
According to the way the dice had rolled.
Years on, young zealots jostle to enlist.
They want adventure, freely cast the die.
And one at least was careless of the cost,
So eagerly he looked towards the sky.
He yearned to fly, he had no thought of war.
He'd meet the perfect girl, he'd drive her wild
And prove himself indeed a man, and there
He's in a wheelchair, coddled, mute, a child.

This silent witness to the shame of war
Perhaps a lion was, or just a lamb.
An Open Day, scarce a year before
Had moved his mind with that recruiting flam.
Now hell or heaven's made within that place,
Impenetrable, private as the tomb.
One hopes his eager dreams still fill that space,
One fears lest nightmares haunt that sombre room.
Or does he muse, and rue he threw the die
Impatient of the minute it would take,
While dazzled by the sunlight in his eye,
To weigh the odds, and ponder on his stake?

The Dream

He stepped, middle-aged, into a trench at Ypres,
Startled, the young-old faces turned to stare.
Wary, unsmiling, the sleep-hungry faces
Turned to him there.
'Where is my father and my son's grandfather?'
He asked, in the hush that had fallen around.
'There are no old men here. Only young men
Under the ground',
One said, and he heard a forgotten cadence,
Turning, he saw the familiar face, alive,
That he had known as a photograph only,
Since he was five.

Of Poets Dead from War

Consider names of poets dead from war.
Thomas, Owen, Rosenberg,
Lewis, Douglas, Apollinaire.
In field, canal, jungle, ditch,
or hospital behind the lines.
Some had posted verses to wives
and mothers the day before;
one in a diary noted
'no more singing for the bird'.

Another wrote 'le ciel est etoile par
les obus des Boches', and printed
poems in violet ink
to circulate among his battery.
A letter ends 'sorry I have to go'.
Gone, young men's faces decorate
the books they never saw of poems
kids read in school.

Near Arras dust-whitened summer roads
remind the tourist racing
for ferry boat and home,
with neat inscriptions on sidelong lanes
of cemeteries immaculate,
of voices lost, things unfulfilled.
Consider for a moment
poets dead from war.

ROY ASHWELL

*Obituaries in the **Times** for 14th October
(the anniversary of the battle of Passchendaele)*

Rocca, Driver, Robertson. Do you hear me
Read your names from the *Times* at nine a.m.
This pelting Wednesday? I fish you from the dark.

Before I was born you were engaged to death,
She bedded you at Passchendaele, undid
Your manhood with the red mouth of a moment's lust.

A gravelong silence answers me, empties the heart,
Freezes the womb to think of you undone
And undone the generations that you left

To march across a century dense with anniversaries.
Your black names massed in the morning columns
Confound the orphaned sense.

The high wet wind cries out; and other histories
Return: the hulks that once were ships, shot ripped
Among the shoals and sea birds calling on the drowned

In the slow spin of the bloody whirlpool we say is Time.
And I remember the wet earth turning over you, undone.
And again the silent intervening years
You might have walked in and all who were not
Your daughters and your sons. Rocca, Driver, Robertson.

PETER BAUM

In 1914 there was a rainbow

In 1914 there was a rainbow.
Black birds swooped, pigeons shone
Silver as they wheeled in circles
Between the grey clouds and a narrow strip of sun.

Battle upon battle. They lied like troopers.
Horrible, those rows of smashed-up heads!
Shells keep on and on exploding,
Losing speed as they tumble.
The arc of pain expands and expands.

Caught between Death and the rainbow,
They clutch their rifles more firmly,
Spitting at the enemy,
Propping up each other,
Tumbling like waves of the sea.
Look! Across the hills they stagger,
Attracted by Death, magnetically.

translated by Merryn Williams

EDMUND BLUNDEN

To W.O. and His Kind

If even you, so able and so keen,
And master of the business you reported
Seem now almost as though you had never been,
And in your simple purpose nearly thwarted,
What hope is there? What harvest from those hours
Deliberately, and in the name of truth,
Endured by you? Your witness moves no Powers,
And younger youth resents your sentient youth.

You would have stayed me with some parable,
The grain of mustard seed, the boy that thrust
His arm into the leaking dike to quell
The North Sea's onrush. Would you were not dust.
With you I might invent, and make men try,
Some genuine shelter from this frantic sky.

(1939)

To Wilfred Owen
(killed in action November 4th 1918)

Where does your spirit walk, kind soldier, now,
In this deep winter, bright with ready guns?
And have you found new poems in this war?

Some would more wish you, with untroubled brow,
Perpetual sleep, which you perhaps wished once -
To unknow this swift return of all you bore.

And yet, if ever in the scheme of things
Past men have leave to see the world they loved,
This night you crossed the lines, for a second seen

By worried sentries. In vast tunnellings
You track the working-party; by the gloved
Wire-sergeant stand; look in at the canteen;

And I, dream-following you, reading your eyes,
Your veteran youthful eyes, discover fair
Some further hope, which did not formerly rise.
Smiling you fade, the future meets you there.

(1940)

VICTORIA BUCKLEY

Scarborough
(for Wilfred Owen)

Can that be the place? There's no view, and it doesn't
have a turret. She points at a sign, that moans softly as it hangs
in the wind, a flapping flag on a wire. Wandering across
the road I have no clear idea what to ask for. The rain falls

silently, not giving anything away. The hotel wears a tired face,
and the proprietress, smiling at first, soon glares. She jerks
a tight, scraped head of hair to the left, and the door slams.
Clearly not a poetry lover. I walk down the hill, watching

the waves leap, feeling a little ridiculous. The building is much
more and much less than I had imagined. Its graceful walls
house the history of Men; but it is peeling away, anxious to
undress, to reveal itself as something modern, more in keeping

with the times. I peer at the turret. The windows are all there,
bespotted spectacles through which the ocean looms large.
I almost see a face. Inside there remains no visible trace of the troops,
and the perky girl at reception claims, after a visible titter,

she's never heard of the man, and in her mind puts me down
as one of those arty types. I inquire whether it's possible to
book the turret room, and wonder at the absence of a visible
plaque. I take my leave quietly, as befitting my mood. Rain

is still falling and it's getting dark. In the car there's a chill, and as
street lights illuminate the way out of Scarborough, a ghost
travels with me, whispering of poetry, slippers, and the dark
nightmare of War, all contained in a room with a view of the sea.

IAN CAWS

The Sambre Canal
(Wilfred Owen: 1893-1918)

It won't be searched for where it may be found,
yet, in the end, there was nothing for him
but the place. He remembered how the ground
at Uffington had been gold, how he'd come
again to hear the ferryman remind
him how private was still water. This time

though, he ignored the French rain, knowing how
the place waited and that it was a place
of water whose compulsion would allow
him nothing. When he walked into its peace,
it was not the peace of buttercups growing from the dawn light. But he might suppose

it, for an instant, no longer searching
in the black water, his feet in the mud.
And when he entered, his hand was touching
a duckboard and there was calm, nothing said
that what he'd found was beyond all reaching
or how cold, how secret, the water stayed.

GLADYS MARY COLES

For the Centenary of Wilfred Owen

In Milton Road tonight, a boy playing in the summer light
wears a crash helmet, manoeuvres his bike.
Down the slope he rides, shoots a frown at me,
aware that I'm staring at Fifty-One -
Victorian villa, the Birkonian home
of the Owens (Tom, Susan, four children).
From here Wilfred, proud of his uniform,
smartly set off to Whetstone Lane, and school.
A time that was nurturing, unriven:
Sunday School at Claughton, walks to Bidston -
woods and windmill he knew well; also Meols
(his cousins' house, 'Dorfold'). For young Harold
brotherly protection, inventions, games.
And boyhood joys – swimming at local Baths,
riding a horse beside wild Mersey waves;
his pleasure in learning, crafting first poems.

Ten years from here, a lifetime further on,
nerves shattered by shell-fire near St. Quentin,
did he, perhaps, think back to Birkenhead,
recall the mothering hours at Milton Road
where a boy, tonight, is riding his bike in the summer light?

N44, France: Holiday Route

Maize, wheat, vines border the road,
a straight road, one hour to Rheims,
this the country of Champagne.
The celebration wine from sad flatlands;
white of the white grape
from a blood-soaked earth.
Signposts are to cemeteries,
graves, as neat and thickly planted
as the rows of vines. No bubbles here,
no sparkle. On one side a crucifix;
on the other, a stone hand holding
a stone flame. A little stone for every man.
War is soil-deep here, though the maize
grows fine ears, the vines have luscious grapes –
all this ground seems tender,
vulnerable. Hardly breathing, not believing
in any harvest, least of all its own.

Yes, there are poppies, still in abundance;
neither are the larks absent, nor their singing.
Yet the peace now lying over this landscape
seems merely a transfer about to be peeled back
to reveal the real scene: battle, ambush.
Trees seem about to explode;
fields, copses, grassy knolls
all units in the strategy, the campaign.

While Mephistopheles drinks champagne
an angel smiles through centuries of war
over the cathedral door
at Rheims, where hotels offer the best of wine
and tourists stay, less to mourn than dine.

MARGARET CRANE

A Drawing Down of Blinds
(Monkmoor Road, Shrewsbury)

There are thousands, perhaps millions, of such houses:
raw redbrick, trimmed with washed-out hydrangeas;
in every town they line Victorian roads
above the railway. The streets beyond are newer:
the roof lines lower. This row must have looked,
in his time, unhindered to Wenlock and the Wrekin.

From black Birkenhead, from desperate shabby-genteel
pretentious poverty, they came to this
clean drowsy town, where Wilfred every evening
sat at his desk in the bay of the attic window,
in the suburban twilight, and thought that nothing
would ever happen.

A few months of the noise,
the responsibility, the limbs in shellholes,
were enough to happen. *Weep, you may weep, for you
may touch them not.* Twilight showed up the corpses
lying in the hollows of the Hampshire downs;
and through a window in Scarborough sent a whisper:
A voice I know: and this time I must go.

Weep, you may weep, for you ... on Armistice Day
the telegraph boy biked up with his envelope, and
the unwilling blinds were drawn as bells swung wildly
among the vanes of Shrewsbury; and each slow dusk
that settled on the street came drifting gently
through the attic window, hoping to find him there.

At the Grave of Wilfred Owen

Ors-sur-Sambre

He who in life was always
out on the edge – the wrong provincial town,
the wrong school, the wrong regiment, even
the wrong kind of love – lies neatly now
out on the edge, behind the leaden line
of the uncrossed canal.

Neither at Ypres nor the Somme, but elsewhere.
The granite pinnacles and plaster flowers
of French civilian graves obscure the corner
of white orderly slabs: two dozen Manchesters
dead over two November days together.
A two-by-four plot of Artois contains him.

He is elsewhere in any case:
where fatuous sunbeams toil; where brambles clutch
and cling with sorrowing hands; where evening brings
a drawing-down of blinds…nearer, or farther,
than Ors, or Shrewsbury: out on the edge
of our uncrossed imaginations.

FRANK DICKINSON

In Memoriam

We see the stone soldier each November.
Hewn from our Bradford flesh, bayonet fixed,
Poised, hunched, as if forever flinching forward
Through some Somme-swept lead-storm.
We stand around, we sing hyms, we match his silence,
Break it with a bugle-call,
                                        Favour his air with flags…

I look at his athletic mien, his fine
Chiselled jawline, his eyes peering onwards,
Sweeping fearfulness from foreign fields,
Fear from our sensibilities…
I cry for a noble weariness
Caught by the sculptor…

…those were my childish thoughts;
I think them still…

Every Boy's Own hero of a lost time
With his neat-bound outtees, tilted helmet,
Bayonet tipped .303 Lee-Enfield rifle
Angled for killing, frail breast tensed
For throwing off speeding lead-nosed bullets
Zipping, sighing by; seeking billets
In eye or throat, or crotch.
A Bradford Pal in Victoria Square forever.

The last one died yesterday;
The last to fall from the untidy muckle
Of men who knew Manningham Park and Ripon Camp;
They climbed sweating, frightened, cursing
Yorkshire style from safety's trench
Into that sunshined, metalled death-mesh

Slowly sieving out, one by one,
The boys from Bradford-Dale.

They showed him serene – a steady stare;
A Bradford face of mill and weft and grist,
Of swaying trams on wearing points,
Of railway horses, spitting gas-lamps
And all the rest that we have learned…

He's gone now; they're all gone;
All time-expired for museums and circumstance.

~ ☆ ☆ ☆ ~

KEITH DOUGLAS

Landscape with Figures (1)

Perched on a great fall of air
a pilot or angel looking down
on some eccentric chart, the plain
dotted with the useless furniture
discerns crouching on the sand vehicles
squashed dead or still entire, stunned
like beetles: scattered wingcases and
legs, heads, show when the haze settles.
But you who like Thomas come
to poke fingers in the wounds
find monuments, and metal posies:
on each disordered tomb
the steel is torn into fronds
by the lunatic explosive.

FREDA DOWNIE

For Wilfred Owen

Today you would find your distant sad shire
Apparently forgetful of slaughtered innocence
And given wholly to the business of spring.
If you were to approach Habberley for instance,

By way of the stream and erratic plovers,
You would meet a girl in a delicate mood
Airing the latest generation in a pram
While carefully avoiding the lane's yeasty mud.

And later, the village dog would confront you
With his oddity of one grey eye and one brown
Dancing attendance on your singularity,
Until you stopped by a cottage almost overgrown

With the season and the gardener's art,
Where even the doorway frames an affair
Of flowers fuming in an old tin helmet
Resigned to being always suspended there.

GERRIT ENGELKE

To the Soldiers of the Great War

Rise up! Out of trenches, muddy holes, bunkers, quarries!
Up out of mud and fire, chalk dust, stench of bodies!
Off with your steel helmets! Throw your rifles away!
Enough of this murderous enmity!

Do you love a woman? So do I.
And have you a mother? A mother bore me.
What about your child? I too love children.
And the houses reek of cursing, praying, weeping.

Were you at ruined Ypres? I was there too.
At stricken Mihiel? I was opposite you.
I was there at Dixmuide surrounded by floods,
At hellish Verdun, in the smoke and the crowds,
Freezing, demoralised, in the snow,
At the corpse-ridden Somme I was opposite you.
I was facing you everywhere, but you did not know it!
Body is piled on body. Poet kills poet.

I was a soldier. I did my job.
Thirsty, sick, yawning, on the march or on guard,
Surrounded by death and missing home –
And you – were your feelings so unlike mine?
Tear open your tunic! Let's see your bare skin;
I know that old scar from 1915,
And there on your forehead the stitched-up gash.
But so you won't think my pain is less,
I open my shirt, here's my discoloured arm!
Aren't we proud of our wounds, your wounds and mine?

You did not give better blood or greater force,
And the same churned-up sand drank our vital juice.
Did your brother die in the blast of that shell?
Did your uncle or your classmate fall?
Does not your bearded father lie in his grave?
Hermann and Fritz, my cousins, bled to death.
And my young, fair-haired friend, always helpful and good,
His home is still waiting, and his bed.
His mother has waited since 1916,
Where is his cross and his grave?
                                                    Frenchmen,
Whether from Bordeaux, Brest, Garonne;
Ukrainian, Turk, Serb, Austrian;
I appeal to all soldiers of the Great War -
American, Russian, Britisher -
You were brave men. Now throw away national pride.
The green sea is rising. Just take my hand.

translated by Merryn Williams

ROGER GARFITT

from *Border Songs*

His last company

halted
against the shade
of a last hill

men he has led

through barrages
posted on fire-steps
huddled with in dugouts

watched and watched over

until their blasphemies
have become
a kind of prayer

all that is human

all he can hear of hope
beneath *the shrill*
demented choirs

no glory in them

only a kind of prayer
he says over and over
all the courage he needs

to break ranks

The Haunting
'What passing-bells for these who die as cattle?'

Only the wash
of their voices
on the air

the singing
from troop-train windows
as they were shipped south

young men in their first flush

    'Quicker their blood to earth
than to their wedding'

who left the ghost-cuts
of their spades
in the potato patch

glimmerings of twine
around raspberry canes
and pea sticks

the shine of their boots
on the roots
of the blackthorn

    'After the revelling
there was silence'.

a stilled voice
in the brimming
of the waterbutt

a stopped hand
in the rust
on the gatelatch

a lost stride
in the greening
of the wheelrut

    The dead were walking
with the walking wounded

                their hands hollowed
                in the hands
                around a match

                their lips drawn
                in the lips drawing
                on the flame

                their hunger crowding
                to the brink
                of the least thing

        and she wove a woman
        from the flower of men

        supple as their hands
        at the lambing, as their wrists
        on the scythe

        light as their step
        on the haycart, as their pitching
        of sheaves

        direct as the line
        of their furrow, as their speech
        among themselves

       and set her to dance
on the potato patch

with the quicksilver
of the otter
before the poles cross

with the side-steps
of the hare
before she's worn down

with the heel-springs
of the deer
until the heart gives out.

DESMOND GRAHAM

Gloucester

I saw all the dead
of the First World War
streaming out of Gloucester Cathedral,
straw in their hair,
a burr in their voices,
singing songs from Percy Grainger
and Sharp, and at Charing Cross
the cockneys met them,
sequins on khaki,
limbers painted red and gold,
their handles dipped
in recognition, from Dorchester
and Newbury,
from Billingsgate and Stepney,
all of them singing,
the young pup of an officer
keeping them straight,
keeping their lines straight
as another crowd
from tenements in Manchester,
Oldham, Leeds or Dewsbury joined them,
and I knew none of their voices,
as Edward Thomas was waving
them past and on
and an old man fingering
medals on his jacket,
and Wilfred Owen, with a hole
the size of a silver threepence
right through his forehead,
Rosenberg waist-deep
in mud stood for a moment

two figures in uniform
one hand on each shoulder
forcing him down,
and Ivor Gurney strode past
calling 'Beethoven
do you see you
as I see you'
and a chorus answered
in nasals and umlauts
all backwards
then rain
splattered the roof
followed by silence.

~ ☆ ☆ ☆ ~

MICHAEL GRAYER

War Without End
(Iraq, November 2000)

'How many miles to Babylon?'
Along an Ancient road, well worn,
Soft winds blow poisoned dust, unseen.
No taste or smell, a cancer upon
The final victim, not yet born.
War without end, Obscene!

JIM GREENHALF

Expression of War Experience

(*The ghost of Wilfred Owen stammers the following poem, which opens at Napier University. The sounds of university life form a background to Owen's monologue. He traverses the grounds and buildings remembering Craiglockhart and his time in the trenches*).

Siegfried called it Dottyville,
but this dull billet
was my university.
I do not recognise the faces
I see now: young men
unravaged or numbed
by multitudinous murders.
I see what I might have become.

The lad from Shropshire,
the parson's agnostic assistant,
the Flying Corps flop,
the infantryman
blown into the air
by a random whizz-bang.
Landing here
        I found my feet.

Unshod by Army issue,
they were warm and always dry.
I missed the spring offensive,
the tongueless mouths of mud
that swallowed men wholesale
at Ypres, and Passchendaele.
Without even a Blighty
or bar of gold
        to justify my convalescence.
I was lucky, don't ask me why.

Unlike the sodden squaddies,
cornered by hellfire or sucked under
by donkeyloads of kit.
A once-over by an orderly,
shot of Navy Rum, cotton wool
to plug their damaged ears,
then up the line again
to face the music;
muddy duckboards cracking underfoot.
Violet-scented air
turning brass buttons green
burned their faces.
Yellow flares
bent them stumbling
into foul and stinking places,
while I settled myself in a chair,
waiting for a space
nearer the fire.

I left my platoon
in a dark and dangerous wood.
I smelled their blood in Champagne,
the wheatlands of Lorraine.
I dreamed of them often,
saw their faces grinning
back at me in the pierglass.
Station whistles at Waverley
brought them over the top of mailbags.
People must have thought me mad
in my blue armband and white tab.
At cock-crow I heard reveille.

Britain was a smooth illusion,
a bowling green, mocking my presence.
I knew death was waiting,
the hooded nurse behind the screen.
On parole from the wood,
I was not deceived.

My blood waited to escape
through some dark and secret hole.
Paroled but not reprieved.

What's my reputation now,
three-quarters of a century
after my little leaf
joined the khaki compost heap?
Do they think me a realist,
mistaking me for Siegfried?
Do they think of us together,
confusing my lines with his?

Even at his angriest Siegfried
was at home in the world,
never less than himself.
Whereas I, the stammering man
shy with secrets, tried to lose myself
in aesthetics – until I saw the amputees,
the art of prosthetics.

I see them once again,
shells of men whose minds
the dead had ravished,
withdrawn behind silent doors.
Shadows in twilight,
negatives exposed to light.
Deafened and made dumb
by the business of bullets.
I see what I might have become.

I had sixteen months of lies
before love drove me back to hell,
to seek forgiveness in their tortured eyes.

NEIL HALL

Before I get old

Wilfred Owen
Was the poet who had to die,
The man who wrote an anthem
For doomed youth
Could not be expected
To survive the war and end his days
Peacefully, in a home for the elderly.

He couldn't end up
Like Pete Townshend.

TONY HARRISON

The Act
(for Michael Longley and James Simmons)

Newcastle Airport and scarcely 7 a.m.
yet they foot the white line out towards the plane
still reeling (or as if) from last night's FED
or macho marathons in someone's bed.
They scorn the breakfast croissants and drink beer
and who am I to censure or condemn?
I know oblivion's a balm for man's poor brain
and once roistered in male packs as bad as them.
These brews stoke their bravado, numb their fear
but anaesthetise all joy along with pain.

To show they had a weekend cunt or two
they walked as if they'd shagged the whole world stiff.
The squaddies' favourite and much-bandied words
for describing what they'd done on leave to birds
as if it were pub-brawl or DIY
seem to be, I quote, 'bang', 'bash', or 'screw',
if they did anything (a biggish 'if'!)
more than the banter boomed now at the crew
as our plane levels off in a blue sky
along with half-scared cracks on catching syph.

They've lit Full Strengths on DA 141
despite NO SMOKING signs and cabin crew's
polite requests; they want to disobey
because they bow to orders every day.
The soldiers travel pretty light and free
as if they left Newcastle for the sun,
in winter with bare arms that show tattoos.
The stewardesses clearly hate this run,
the squaddies' continuous crude repartee
and constant button pushing for more booze.

I've heard the same crude words and smutty cracks
and seen the same lads on excursion trains
going back via ferry from Stranraer
queuing at breakfast at the BR bar,
cleaning it out of Tartan and Brown Ale.
With numbered kitbags piled on luggage racks
just after breakfast bombed out of their brains,
they balance their empty cans in wobbly stacks.
An old woman, with indulgence for things male,
smiles at them and says, 'They're nobbut wains!'

Kids, mostly cocky Geordies and rough Jocks
with voices coming straight out of their boots,
the voices heard in newsreels about coal
or dockers newly dumped onto the dole
after which the army's the next stop.
One who's breakfasted on Brown Ale cocks
a nail-bitten, nicotined right thumb, and shoots
with loud saliva salvos a red fox
parting the clean green blades of some new crop
planted by farm families with old roots.

A card! The stewardesses almost throw it
into our laps not wanting to come near
to groping soldiers. We write each fact
we're required to enter by 'The Act':
profession; place of birth; purpose of visit.
The rowdy squaddy, though he doesn't know it
(and if he did he'd brand the freak as 'queer'),
is sitting next to one who enters 'poet'
where he puts 'Forces'. But what is it?
My purpose? His? *What* are we doing here?

Being a photographer seems bad enough.
God knows the catcalls that a poet would get!
Newcastle-bound for leave the soldiers rag
the press photographer about his bag
and call him Gert or Daisy, and all laugh.
They shout at him in accents they'd dub 'pouf'
Yoo hoo, hinny! Like your handbag pet!
Though what he's snapped has made him just as tough
and his handbag hardware could well photograph
these laughing features when they're cold and set.

I don't like the thought of these lads manning blocks
but saw them as you drove me to my flight,
now khakied up, not kaylied but alert,
their minds on something else than Scotch or skirt,
their elbows bending now to cradle guns.
The road's through deep green fields and wheeling flocks
of lapwings soaring, not the sort of sight
the sentry looks for in his narrow box.
'Cursed be dullards whom no cannon stuns'
I quote. They won't read what we three write.

They occupy NO SMOKING seats and smoke,
commandos free a few days from command
which cries for licence and I watch them cram
anything boozeable, Brown Ale to Babycham,
into their hardened innards, and they drain
whisky/ lemonade, Bacardi/ Coke,
double after double, one in either hand,
boys' drinks spirit-spiked for the real *bloke!*
Neither passengers nor cabin crew complain
as the squaddies keep on smoking as we land.

And as the morning Belfast plane descends
on Newcastle and one soldier looks,
with tears, on what he greets as 'Geordie grass'
and rakes the airport terrace for 'wor lass'
and another hollers to his noisy mates
he's going to have before their short leave ends
'firkins of fucking FED, fantastic fucks!'
I wish for you, my Ulster poet friends,
pleasures with no rough strife, no iron gates,
and letter boxes wide enough for books.

The Cycles of Donji Vakuf

We take emerald to Bugojno, then the opal route
to Donji Vakuf, where Kalashnikovs still shoot
at retreating Serbs or at the sky
to drum up the leaden beat of victory.
Once more, though this time Serbian, homes
get pounded to facades like honeycombs.
This time it's the Bosnian Muslims' turn
to cleanse a taken town, to loot, and burn.
Donji Vakuf fell last night at 11.
Victory is signalled by firing rounds to heaven
and for the god to whom their victory's owed.
We see some victors cycling down the road
on bikes that they're too big for. They feel so tall
as victors, all conveyances seem small,
but one, whose knees keep bumping on his chin,
rides a kid's cycle, with a mandolin,
also childish size, strapped to the saddle,
jogging against him as he tries to pedal.
His machine-gun and the mandolin impede
his furious pedalling, and slow down the speed
appropriate to victors, huge-limbed and big-booted,
and he's defeated by the small bike that he's looted.

The luckiest looters come down dragging cattle,
two and three apiece, they've won in battle.
A goat whose udder seems about to burst
squirts out her milk to quench a victor's thirst
which others quench with shared beer, as a cow,
who's no idea she's a Muslim's now,
sprays a triumphal arch of piss across
the path of her new happy Bosnian boss.
Another struggles with stuffed rucksack, gun, and bike,
small and red, he knows his kid will like,
and he hands me his Kalashnikov to hold
to free his hands. Rain makes it wet and cold.
When he's balanced his booty, he makes off,
for a moment, forgetting his Kalashnikov,
which he slings with all his looted load
onto his shoulder and trudges down the road,
where a solitary reaper passes by,
scythe on his shoulder, wanting fields to dry,
hoping, listening to the thunder, that the day
will brighten up enough to cut his hay.

And tonight some small boy will be glad
he's got the present of a bike from soldier dad,
who braved the Serb artillery and fire
to bring back a scuffed red bike with one flat tyre.
And, among the thousands fleeing north, another,
with all his gladness gutted, with his mother,
knowing the nightmare they are cycling in,
will miss the music of his mandolin.

NICK HASLAM

So

You whisper softly and then you lean.
Brief the arrangement, easily met.
A tongue of gold for sniper's snare.

Time: a ration quickly consumed.
Low in the east bloodied banners unfurl,
Slumbering civilians go undisturbed.
As ghosts, we fade from Shadwell Stair.

You caress the scar upon my cheek,
'A blighty once', I murmur.
Under Half Moon sated we drowse,
Folded together in sleepy arms.

Flickering glory now made huge,
Blinded by the candle's light.
Soft are the lips that cup tear-loaded eyes,
Sweet is the passion that burns.

PAULINE HAWKESWORTH

The Gas

They thought you were safe,
had come through the war
without the cold baggage others
carried.

A stretcher bearer
rather than wear a white feather
brave they said,
a front line man.

Ten years it took for mustard gas
to demolish that strong brain,
ten years of headaches
and confusions.

It clawed at you,
just when you thought
you were safe –
that cold baggage others carried
was around your shoulders,
and you were forced to unpack.

~ ☆ ☆ ~

SEAMUS HEANEY

The Party

Overheard at the party, like wet snow
That slumps down off a roof, the unexpected,
Softly powerful name of Wilfred Owen.
Mud in your eye. Artillery in heaven.

NORTON HODGES

At Craiglockhart
(after the film 'Regeneration')

Rivers keeps a Buddha on his night table,
aide-memoire that the world is on fire.

The good Austrian doctor
offered c-c-consolation,
or at least a return to
ordinary unhappiness.

But these boys scream in the dark
from visitations of eyeballs, guts.

At 3 a.m., another cannibal lulled to rest,
he's racked by
the brutal efficiency of the electrical cure.

Even Owen and Sassoon,
drafting, redrafting in the garden,
were primed to return, when his fumbling was done,
to the heaps of flesh where they were kings.

Then Owen crossing a canal,
Sassoon by a whisker.

At dawn he pleads with
that bloody half-smile:

What can I embrace if not my fear?

GEOFFREY HOLLOWAY

Wilfred Owen

An updated Shropshire lad,
you moved into the blinds, old son,
bridge-building a week too soon.
One more doomed youth. Hard luck, hard lead.

~ ☆ ☆ ☆ ~

STEPHEN HORSFALL

To Wilfred Owen

Glory's the lie war's cancer feeds upon,
You said. You told the truth – that war is hell,
But now the guns are still. Your task is done.

The tales of glory that the old men spun
You showed as lies – you broke their hateful spell.
Glory's the lie war's cancer feeds upon.

For all the dead, destroyed by gas or gun,
Yours was the voice that questioned why they fell,
But now the guns are still. Your task is done.

War was the enemy, and not the Hun.
No glorious combat: gangrene, gas and shell.
Glory's the lie war's cancer feeds upon.

The gun that spat your hasty orison
Could never kill the bitter truth you tell,
But now the guns are still. Your task is done:

And when the final war on death is won
The unnumbered dead will have their passing-bell.
Glory remains the lie war feeds upon,
And other guns boom still: our task goes on.

PETER HOWARD

A Poppy

We went into a village where violets had just broken out.
Snipers were exchanging samphire,
and there were scenes of carnation everywhere.
I saw someone running with a bunch of live geraniums.
Suddenly there was a burst of chrysanthemum,
and honeysuckle crackled along the hedgerows.
Children were covered in crocus and bluebells;
there were old men waving ancient ivy.
Those unable to arm themselves with daffodils
made do with tulips, cyclamen, anything they could lay their
    hands on.
Then we heard that a buttercup had landed on the hospital.
We rushed to the scene: patients were emerging, dahlia and lilac,
some with periwinkle or lesser celandine.
It was jasmine. All I could think was 'Is there no myrtle?
When will common hawthorn prevail?'
But there was nothing we could do but willow and broom.
By the end of the day there were hundreds lying on makeshift
    beds of roses.

> *Lamium,*
> *Pyracantha, Euphorbia gorgonis,*
> *Viola tricolor, Aconitum napellus,*
> *Amaranthus caudatus,*
> *Yucca aloifolia, Yucca gloriosa,*
> *Salix babylonica,*
> *Artemisia**

And afterwards the generals awarded themselves petals.

---

* Deadnettle, Firethorn, Gorgon's head, Heartsease, Helmet flower, Love-lies-bleeding, Spanish bayonet, Spanish dagger, Weeping willow, wormwood.

TED HUGHES

Wilfred Owen's Photographs

When Parnell's Irish in the House
Pressed that the British Navy's cat
O-nine-tails be abolished, what
Shut against them? It was
Neither Irish nor English nor of that
Decade, but of the species.

Predictably, Parliament
Squared against the motion. As soon
Let the old school tie be rent
Off their necks, and give thanks, as see gone
No shame but a monument –
Trafalgar not better known.

'To discontinue it were as much
As ship not powder and cannonballs
But brandy and women'. (Laughter). Hearing which
A witty profound Irishman calls
For a 'cat' into the House, and sits to watch
The gentry fingering its stained tails.

Whereupon ....
        quietly, unopposed,
The motion was passed.

KIT JACKSON

Photograph

Where next?
I search your face for clues,
your dark eyes haunt,
blank, opaque,
making no contact...
and yet – is it illusion?
there *is* something...

You raise your head,
gaze gravely into the lens,
seeing Uncle Gunston's hand
holding the camera steady.
You stand immaculate:
the perfect officer cadet,
outwardly composed –
and yet thinking... what?

The shutter opens

and in that moment
your image
floated over a century
engages me:
one among the years
studying your face
your uncle saw
through the aperture
of his camera. Instantly

The shutters open.

JASIM

(Child poet of Iraq, 1985-1998)

Identity Card

The name is Love,
The class is Mindless,
The governorate is Sadness,
The city is Sighing,
The home number is
One Thousand Sighs.

MIKE JENKINS

Mad Jack Spoils V.E. Day

We done ower ouse up lovely
like er 'ighness woz visitin,
planned t'ave a barbeque party
with Fancy Dress wartime clothin.

Not on-a Close isself, mind yew,
thisint Balaclava nor Kashmir Street
we've risen above all that:
jest invited the selected few.

The Murphys from up-a Close
an-a S4C's down-a way ....
didn' wan' non o' theyr abuse,
'ey could bugger off f' VE Day.

Wore my dad's ol medals,
my missis wuz Vera Lynn,
my boy Ben wuz-a S.A.S. corporal
looked great with is plastic gun.

The bonfire wuz stacked up tidy
like Guy Fawkes all over agen.
Ower guests wuz Churchill, Spitfire pilots, Monty,
neighbours we ardly knew become friends.

Witch 'cross-a street come as a char
(could even stand er voice tha day),
"appy V.D. Day!' says she with a larf.
'More like 'alloween!' I wuz 'bout t' say.

Then in-a jungle eat of-a barbeque
arf-pissed an singin 'Slong way t' Tipperary'
'is weird bloke comes up t' me,
lookin like ee wuz goin t' spew.

~ 46 ~

'Yew new round yer?' I asked suspicious.
'I've just returned to peruse the scene'.
Ee shot me down with a real posh tone
(SS the initials on is cigarette case).

Ee lit up an I thought 'Ow sick!'
'So where have you fought, old man?'
ee queried an I felt like a dick
(neally said The Vulcan an Buffaloes down town!).

Tha's when I knew ee woz a schizo,
some psycho out on Community Care:
babbled on 'bout flingin is medal in-a river
an ow a tank ud soon come by yer.

Ee even talked in bloody Latin,
arpin on 'bout some bloke Owen.
I smiled polite an arst is name,
'Siegfned' ee says .... might o' known!

I wen off an let im alone,
friend of-a Murphys most problee
come t' spoil ower fun:
Queen Mum on TV raisin er and gracious, never armin no-one.

But when-a two minutes silence come
tha total nutter of a man
ee arrives in a stolen tipper truck,
caused chaos, didn give a fuck.

Down ower drive sent tables an buntin flyin,
toppled ower grill yellin 'bout Music 'alls.
I phoned 999, tol em an excaped German
wuz on-a loose: 'ey thought I wuz talkin balls.

Mrs. Boreman opposite threw frankies at im
like and-grenades aimin,
all-a rest ran in-a ouse shit scared,
I shouted 'The police're comin!' from upstairs.

When ee'd flattened enough, ee went on.
In-a 'Merthyr' nex week the eadlines read
MAD JACK SPOILS VE DAY CELEBRATIONS!!
Know wha? Ee wuz a soldier oo'd turned out bard!

I reckon them Murphys or Llewellyns ired im,
coz apparently ee ewsed t' write poetree.
An if ee'd bin a soldier surely ee'd-a known
that all-a tewns 'n' booze 'n' steaks wuz f' victree.

DENYS L. JONES

Cain in the Jungle

I have killed my brother in the jungle;
Under the green liana's clammy tangle
I hid, and pressed my trigger, and he died.

Smooth as the spotted panther crept my brother,
Never a creak of his equipment's leather,
Never a leaf dislodged nor bird offended.

With his palaeozoic prototype
My mother shared her own ungainly shape
In caverns on some slow Silurian stream;

And with the cublings played my father's sons,
Shoulder to shoulder chipped their flints and bones
Or scraped a greasy ichthyosaurus hide.

And, when the floods of purple slime receded
My brother's hutments by the apes were raided,
I lay beneath my brother's legs and cried.

Yet I have fought my brother for the planets;
I have never stopped to hear the linnets,
Or watch the cocos grow against the moon.

I have only slain him in the shadows,
I have made his slant-eyed women widows
And inherited his empty meadows.

JUDITH KAZANTZIS

For example Owen

A question to four deaths:
Wilfred Owen, France 1918
Ernst Tauber, France 1918
David Tinker, off the Falklands 1982
Armando Souda, off the Falklands 1982

An officer, a good shepherd
who thought he should go
with his doomed flock, with love.
He asked, how could he sit in comfort
even in conscience and inside prison
while his men passed in their thousands
under the hand of the giant into the cave.
So he went back in there. He 'went west'.
A bullet smashed him on a canal bank
a week before Armistice.
The very bridge (over the Sambre)
was never built that his men
tried to build. Almost all of them
were 'casualties'. He was 'struck'
while 'calmly' helping to fix the
duckboards into place. There,
Owen handed himself into the war.
He 'fell' among planks awash,
hit and hit, smashed, gouged into
springing arrowhead shards under
the fire; by virtue of a crafty
self-deceit, by reason of a huge desire
for a virtuous reason to live, out of purest
nobility; among debris slithering
across Lethe, planks drifting waterlogged
and sideways, batted by each other,

nudged by shapes hunched underwater
like giants; he fell down among
matchsticks carrying the random and
slumped dead making a crossing.
Planks for white crosses
like plague signs stuck up forever
and tended, as if the crushing plague
might lift, one day, from our houses
if the signs are kept fresh
and we remember.

We don't forget.
The lethal courage of the lamb.
Our bloodgeld two wars long.
From old colonial days
a malaria flickers underskin
a muttering sootfall
of sorrow and love, hate and revenge
upworded to the old noble
pro patria decorum est...... . Gasbag
speeches unworded to the pure brass blare
of Downing Street. Upcoding into
computers, signals, radar, rockets, missiles
and three torpedoes
to hit, hit, hit
'a likely violation of the exclusion zone'.

By Sambre
they hadn't invented bodybags
with plastic zips. Stretchers they had.

'All a poet can do today is warn'.
With what caught pride does the young
officer draw up to his peaked cap.
In the photograph
Owen smiles with his expressive
eyes and his plump cheeks. In the next,

~ 51 ~

a glad, rangy face, fair hair,
David Tinker, Lieut. RN, on board, ploughing
the South Atlantic, at first ardent,
then writing home, 'the professional forces
of both sides' – he was one -
'do what they are told. If two
megalomaniac idiots tell them
to beat each other's brains out they do'.
A week later an Exocet
'beat its way' to his cruiser.
Among those burned to death was Tinker.
'To the end he was calm and brave'.
Tinker, David... soldier, sailor. Souda, Armando.
Tauber, Ernst. Owen, Wilfred. Smiles. Rictus.
Caught in smiles, some. Zipped up.
Flown home to a salute. Interred. Crossed white.
With what ritual pride does the young
officer draw up to his peaked cap.

'My subject is War and the pity
of war'... Owen
Tinker... Tauber... Souda.
O passionate lovers of the public virtue
O young wisemen of pity,
how is it, deftly, deftly, you kill
but yourselves only? The flatterers
salute you out.

You golden fleecy flock, why run
before the brokers and the farmers of blood?
They buy and sell in tender carcasses
on war's slab, and in between
in peace – they speculate in futures.
While the young rams breed up
glittering with a hard urge to wrestle death.

The flatterers have released you
among the stumps of French woods or on
sheep islands among cavelike seas -
Here are the high-powered assault rifles,
the heat-sensing missiles entirely
under your hands -
Turn around, look round behind you.
See them sitting comfortably behind you
in their bunkers, on silk chairs.
There they work.
They sail corpses like paper boats.
Make another formation, brothers -
Lock your sights – Advance
on these rears – satiny rear ends.
Your words become your weapons, your weapons
are your words; licking across the ceremonial grounds:
breaking to the rear: No more!
     No more your burden beasts!
     Our missiles stuff your arses
     so no more death trumpeting and trumpeting.

So say it to your flatterers.

Turn, soldiers of unfreedom, look round.
We who love you, who are your own people
we offer a docile back-up
to those who farm your deaths -
Turn and curse us
out of our timidly ranked houses
from which we offer you up.

But you say: Orders are orders.
But you say: I cannot leave my men, my brothers.
But you say: Now this is my only life
    so has to be my death.
    No one at home can know our deep bonds.

I shout back through the dumb wood
across the bloody channels:

You are the soldiers, not them.
Envisage a life, not a death
in brotherhood – is that impossible to men?
This question is for you.
You are tied to a killing post by garlands
marvellous and phantom as poems.
Whip vines or gossamer, what garland ties
you to your killing post?
Which one, steel or breakable?
This question is for you.

Owen... Tauber... Tinker... Souda
it was the question I burned to ask
of the brave shepherds, the brave sheep, dead mutton.

GREVEL LINDOP

The Legacy: Emmer Green, 1956

Let the boy try. The chisel's edge is slid
into the crack. A few businesslike knocks
should do it. Gently now. The blistered lid
resists, resists. He levers at the box,

I hold it steady. All day long they've worked
to sort Miss Mary's things. A magpie-nest
of clothes, toys, jewellery, papers, bills, that lurked
in bags, chests, cupboards, clocks; and with the rest

I'm told, the poet's letters, stuffed in absurd
odd corners. They asked *us* to have a go
at these old trunks and crates. Why she left word
the Scouts should open this, I'll never know.

A splintering crack. It gives. A musty cover
of cloth, and under it the dull green
nubbed bulk of a fully-loaded revolver.
Army issue. Nineteen-seventeen.

Thirty corroded live rounds in a pouch
of mouldy leather. Gasping, the lads crowd in.
Treasure-trove! No. No: better not touch.
Steadying my hands, I pack the things again.

In mildewed lint and sour buttery tarnish
the huge unwieldy ghost of war is laid.
My fingers nearly slip on the dull varnish.
Lifting the box, I learn that I'm afraid.

KATHLEEN LIVERSIDGE

7 Borage Lane, Ripon
(in search of Wilfred Owen)

They've changed the modest face of No 7.
Replaced roof pantiles, put an unseemly window in
The room below his attic,
Removed a memorial plaque, the house being up for sale,
But kept the garden cottagey.
Old pavings curve within an arc of wall,
Continue to the door:
He must have trod them scores of times through May
And into June's high summer of '18,
Coming from camp beside the leaf-dark stream,
Seen these old roots of lily of the valley flower,
Moss roses on the gateway bower in bloom
And mint grown tall and pungent, as today.

Was it mere chance late owners have retained
THE SKYLIGHT? Spared the significant, the looked-for thing
Identified with him?
Maybe a preservation order served to stay
The improving hand?
Near history's ironies, the claims of popular mores,
Posterity (our theme-park culture's heir)
Might, like as not, be eager to extract
From glistening panes
A token 'heritage' tear-drop, packaged as a sop
To all those nagging past and present shames, and wars.

Yet, above all, and in despite,
The sky-reflecting glass lets in the light,
The clarities he saw.

MICHAEL LONGLEY

The War Graves

The exhausted cathedral reaches nowhere near the sky
As though behind its buttresses wounded angels
Snooze in a halfway house of gargoyles, rainwater
By the mouthful, broken wings among pigeons' wings.

There will be no end to clearing up after the war
And only an imaginary harvest-home where once
The Germans drilled holes for dynamite, for fieldmice
To smuggle seeds and sow them inside these columns.

The headstones wipe out the horizon like a blizzard
And we can see no farther than the day they died,
As though all of them died together on the same day
And the war was that single momentous explosion.

Mothers and widows pruned these roses yesterday,
It seems, planted sweet williams and mowed the lawn
After consultations with the dead, heads meeting
Over this year's seed catalogues and packets of seeds.

Around the shell holes not one poppy has appeared,
No symbolic flora, only the tiny whitish flowers
No one remembers the names of in time, brookweed
And fairy flax, say, lamb's lettuce and penny-cress.

In mine craters so vast they are called after cities
Violets thrive, as though strewn by each cataclysm
To sweeten the atmosphere and conceal death's smell
With a perfume that vanishes as soon as it is found.

At the Canadian front line permanent sandbags
And duckboards admit us to the underworld, and then
With the beavers we surface for long enough to hear
The huge lamentations of the wounded caribou.

Old pals in the visitors' book at Railway Hollow
Have scribbled 'The severest spot. The lads did well'
'We came to remember' and the woodpigeons too
Call from the wood and all the way from Accrington.

I don't know how Rifleman Parfitt, Corporal Vance,
Private Costello of the Duke of Wellingtons,
Driver Chapman, Topping, Atkinson, Duckworth,
Dorrell, Wood come to be written in my diary.

For as high as we can reach we touch-read the names
Of the disappeared, and shut our eyes and listen to
Finches' chitters and a blackbird's apprehensive cry
Accompanying Charles Sorley's monumental sonnet.

We describe the comet at Edward Thomas's grave
And, because he was a fisherman, that headlong
Motionless deflection looks like a fisherman's fly,
Two or three white after-feathers overlapping.

Geese on sentry duty, lambs, a clattering freight-train
And a village graveyard encompass Wilfred Owen's
Allotment, and there we pick from a nettle bed
One celandine each, the flower that outwits winter.

BRIAN PATTEN

The Brackets

I look down the contents list at the poets' names -
de la Mare (1873-1956)
Farjeon (1881-1965)
Graves (1895-1985).

I look down the list then stop,
Then look up again at one sandwiched between
These benign octogenarians -
Owen (1893-1918).

At first it seems unfair,
Twenty-five, then gone. Hard to believe
I drank beneath the stars with one
Who crouched beneath the light from flack with him,

Or that in my teens I'd briefly met
A woman who had known
His beauty and his awkwardness.
Now she too is bone.

No longer the youngest on the contents list
The names of friends crop up.
Some are gone.
Tumour-ridden, the brackets close in.

They drop against the ends of names,
Not orderly, but any old how.
Henri, Mitchell, McGough – watch it, mates,
The brackets, any day now.

JIM QUINN

The Shoe

Tonight the black desert is velvet soft,
With a star-hung powdered sky,
And a searchlight moon to light my way,
To the solitary, squat, latrine.

But I stumble,
And stooping, find the cause,
A tiny and shiny, broken baby's shoe;
I hold it, whilst the artillery flashes,
On its peculiar untactical gloss,
And wonder,
Where is the child,
Who has lost its shoe?

Tonight, while *my* daughter sleeps,
Through blessed distance and ignorance,
I wonder, with such innocence at hand,
By what advance or progress of man,
Has caused the loss,
Of a broken child's shoe.

ALAN RHYS-THOMPSON

Sonnet in Half-Rhyme

With love of beauty, eagerness for love,
You wore your youth and ventured into hell;
Not loath, perhaps, but how could it survive
Where grass, soil, trees became one cratered whole?

You saw and, seeing, spoke; you saw for those
Who fought and cursed and feared their way through war.
You spoke when they could not, and felt that this
Was what your vision and your mission were.

But still you sought for beauty and you found
It strangely verdant in the blood and mire;
You held it, told it, but you never feigned
To think that life at best was nothing more.

You still call down the century's warring years,
Invoking 'reciprocity of tears'.

DAPHNE ROCK

Death Assemblage

Ploughing the Somme fields
year after year the corn
full-headed, ears fat and prosperous,
blades throwing
a bleached bone, a splinter
distorted with rust which has bled
and crusted into a metal scab.

Now they have exposed a mass grave
of assorted bone. Buttons
bulbous with accretions.
It makes the six o'clock news:
the authorities
are concerned to discover
whether like lies with like
and who can be named
with his regimental buttons,
his vestigial shoulder tabs.

Millions of years past
the mountains shifted, swept
dead shell to rock grave,
ammonite and brachiopod, crinoid,
they died apart
and then brushed shoulders, landed fixed
immutably with strangers.
Geologists label this
a death assemblage

The authorities are busy
counting buttons, scraping off
deposits, sorting and dividing.
How many buttons make man?

Say six. That means
plots must be cleared for twenty-eight found men.
Perhaps the hearts
of some descendants can be cheered,
grandad found at last. But dead.
Of course research may show
a shell-disturbed collection,
may include
the enemy; our boys beside the Hun.
A death assemblage.

VERNON SCANNELL

The Great War

Whenever war is spoken of
I find
The war that was called Great invades the mind:
The grey militia marches over land
A darker mood of grey
Where fractured tree-trunks stand
And shells, exploding, open sudden fans
Of smoke and earth.
Blind murders scythe
The deathscape where the iron brambles writhe;
The sky at night
Is honoured with rosettes of fire,
Flares that define the corpses on the wire
As terror ticks on wrists at zero hour.
These things I see,
But they are only part
Of what it is that slyly probes the heart:
Less vivid images and words excite
The sensuous memory
And, even as I write,
Fear and a kind of love collaborate
To call each simple conscript up
For quick inspection:
Trenches' parapets
Paunchy with sandbags; bandoliers, tin-hats,
Candles in dug-outs,
Duckboards, mud and rats.
Then, like patrols, tunes creep into the mind:
*A Long, Long Trail, The Rose of No-Man's Land,
Home Fires* and *Tipperary;*
And through the misty keening of a band

Of Scottish pipes the proper names are heard
Like fateful commentary of distant guns:
Passchendale, Bapaume, and Loos, and Mons.
And now,
Whenever the November sky
Quivers with a bugle's hoarse, sweet cry,
The reason darkens; in its evening gleam
Crosses and flares, tormented wire, grey earth
Splattered with crimson flowers,
And I remember
Not the war I fought in
But the one called Great
Which ended in a sepia November
Four years before my birth.

~ ☆ ☆ ☆ ~

CHRISTOPHER SOMERVILLE

Saving Owen

Shivering flesh. A quick sharp blow
across the canal. Mist clearing. Aligned
eye, bead and man. Never to know
consequence of his trick; the lightening mind
snuffed to a spark, then out; the energy
dammed at his squeeze. Denying the creator,
fulfilling prophecy. 'I am the enemy
you killed, my friend' – maybe he'll read that, later.

Sergeant: his hand, caught in your crosswires, still,
surest of shots. Your skill can save this day,
start some sad slide, misting of view, crude gay
exposure, perhaps .... Better the kiss and kill
he'll send, clinically battening dark hatches.
Flawed God from hell some kind of Jesus snatches.

JON STALLWORTHY

Goodbye to Wilfred Owen

*killed, while helping his men
bring up duckboards, on the
bank of the Sambre Canal.*

After the hot convulsion, this
cold struggle to break free – from whom?
I am not myself nor are his
hands mine, though once I was at home
with them. Pale hands his mother praised,
nimble at the keyboard, paler
now and still, waiting to be prised
from wood darker for their pallor.

Head down in a blizzard of shrapnel,
before the sun rose we had lost
more than our way. Disembodied
mist moves on the goose-fleshed canal,
dispersing slowly like the last
plumed exhalations of the dead.

A poem about Poems About Vietnam

The spotlights had you covered (thunder
in the wings). In the combat zones
and in the Circle, darkness. Under
the muzzles of the microphones
you opened fire, and a phalanx
of loudspeakers shook on the wall;
but all your cartridges were blanks
when you were at the Albert Hall.

Lord George Byron cared for Greece,
Auden and Cornford cared for Spain,
confronted bullets and disease
to make their poems' meaning plain;
but you – by what right did you wear
suffering like a service medal,
numbing the nerve that they laid bare,
when you were at the Albert Hall?

The poets of another time-
Owen with a rifle-butt
between his paper and the slime,
Donne quitting Her pillow to cut
a quill – knew that in love and war
dispatches from the front are all.
We believe them, they were there,
when you were at the Albert Hall.

Poet, they whisper in their sleep
louder from underground than all
the mikes that hung upon your lips
when you were at the Albert Hall.

EDWARD STOREY

Red Poppy
(for Wilfred Owen)

I will mourn at this moment
only one of the many who claim
my remembrance, one tenant
of the numberless dead who climb
from their drowned and unknown graves
to hear mock bugle-calls
from earth's white cenotaphs.

I wear this flower for him
who walked where Christ had credence among
the unceremonious phlegm
of those who died too soon, or sang
their sad rebukes to leaders
in braid and surplice whose
incense was cordite-strong.

I think only of his cross
carried from trench and hole to a hill
where the pious crowds express
their loud hypocrisies and smell
cold blood in the falling leaves.
From his deserted height
he asks, 'Was it for this?'

I weep today for him and all
he wept for – the innocent and young
led blindly beyond their toil,
who had no eyes for right or wrong
until too late, their first sight gone.
Mourn now their brief, fierce spring
and hear his warning song.

ISOBEL THRILLING

Museum of Artillery at Woolwich

Guns;
thick curves
of polished sunlight,
small boys
stroke the skin of war.

They mouth endearments,
almost feel
each weapon flex its
metal spine;
wiped clean of ghosts
and blood
the shine is sensuous.

The monument above
their heads
has sugared cherubs
blowing plump kisses
over cannon
cut from marble ice.

Death is sinuously forged;
thin blades
of ancient swords excite
desire for thrust
and shape.

Tin soldiers boxed in glass
die for a coin
in-a-slot
among red paint
and cotton-buds of smoke.

The children laugh;
buy postcards at the door.

THERESA TURK

Going to Gallipoli

'I don't want to go to Gallipoli', I said.
'I don't want to be reminded.
I don't want to remember the mule corps
and the long faces under the wide brimmed hats,
that flicker and jerk in the old, brown clip
they show on TV. I don't want to smell the smell
of the waterproof capes and the mud and the lice'.

'Don't look at it that way', said a man in the coach.
'I belong to a War Games club -
this summer we're doing war cemeteries
of Belgium'. I had come for Byzantium
and the mosques and the hot springs of Bursa,
but we got to Cannakale, where the fish gleam
in the Dardanelles and crossed to Gallipoli.

Flaked with sweet almond and wild cherry blossom,
the peninsula rose and fell,
fingering beaches strewn with forgotten
nests of dead sea mines and rusted barbed wire.
We came to the cliff road. No one spoke
in the coach. Below us, suddenly, a blue sea
was there, the waves, long, low, lovely with laughing foam.

After the fighting's done, they always put the dead
in quiet places; the still air
was warm, scented with rosemary and thyme.
Dappled by wind flowers, a cross and a name,
'aged twenty-two – may his soul rest in peace'.
The war games man made notes in a red diary.
Reel after reel the old, brown silent film plays on.

WILLIE VERHEGGHE

As a child dying from bullets

Dead he is, I know, Owen's breath dies
in books, that morning in November,
in some godforsaken dive in France
where many years of weary battling lie
bleeding to death against beheaded trees.

And yet: I see, hear, smell him,
as if he sits writing at my table,
composed, with soft beautiful hands
above yellow paper pleading for words.
He knows I'm at his shoulder and laughs.

Let me howl for him like a wolf,
help me rub the mud from his eyes
and stand by me at his grave
where he lies crying forever.
As a child dying from bullets.

translated by Peter Nijmeijer

JOHN WARD

For Private George Ward, Executed in France for Desertion in Face of the Enemy, September 1914, aged 20.

There could have been worse ways, worse times, to go
So early on, summer still in flower,
the firing squad a quick clean ending.

Spared cohabitation with rats and lice,
spared the stench of gangrenous limbs,
the 'burning faggots' of trench foot.
Later, you might have choked on phosgene,
been butchered from the rear by friendly fire,
slipped off a duckboard and drowned in slime,
or have hung out of reach on barbed wire
in No Man's Land, your screams ripping wide
open some interminable flare-lit night.

There was even a certain dignity
in being condemned by a general,
with trim moustache and polished boots,
nursing his cold fear that you might start
in the lower orders an unwelcome
fashion for flight instead of fight.

You couldn't help walking from the carnage
with other comrades, saying you were hit.
(We know now there are wounds which do not bleed).
Those weekend camps on Salisbury Plain,
flagwaving crowds at departure stations,
bands playing in regimental scarlet
were poor preparation for a blitzkrieg
and the company of corpses
on the roadside in September's dust.

But why of your own freewill did you go back?
Better to have made them hunt you down
like a fox, house to house and farm to farm,
than give them their chance to waste your life.
One name on a memorial looks
very like another, and no one asks
at this late date what kind of death each died.

~ ☆ ☆ ☆ ~

MERRYN WILLIAMS

Viriconium

Eighty-five years is nothing, an imperceptible
blink on the face of the stone god of history.
I say it does not count. Greater stretches of time
have passed, since the Romans abandoned Wroxeter.

Eighty-five years ago saw a student cycle
the long, dusty, carless road from Shrewsbury ;
blue September, the Wrekin as it is today,
dew glistening on the mounds, similar sheep grazing
between the bath-house walls of the ruined city.

This was better than Latin. He scoured the site
for iron keys, a fragment of dark-red pottery,
a coin stamped with the image of the goddess Luna;
urged his brother, think what we may be missing,
the great find of the century!

Some of his finds got into the town museum,
can be seen there in dusty glass containers,
mixed up, not labelled with his name, Wilfred Owen.

The boy picked up his steel horse,
made his way through summer darkness back to Shrewsbury.
School was next day, and war was a barbarous game,
fit only for the Romans.

Wilfred's Bridge
1st November 1998

Shrewsbury flooded. Three of the four roads
out of town blocked, and the Severn steadily rising,
drowning alders, swamping riverside gardens.
Water has wholly cut off the Welsh Bridge;
the English Bridge you can still wade over, on duckboards.
Water enters the little shops, boutiques
and newsagents, seeps into the big wine warehouse
on London road, and bottles are washed from their cellars,
carried out on the tide. On Wilfred's bridge,
you stand and watch them bob along with sticks
and froth, in brief bursts of November light,
giving the dark brown liquid a richer taste,
dirtying the foam. This stream is travelling past
the Norman sandstone abbey, Wilfred's church.
He isn't here. His body is in France.
His name came back, is written on a tablet
high on its walls.

        He never mentioned Shrewsbury.
To him it was reactionary, provincial;
like most young kids, he couldn't wait to get out.
Yet, this weekend, his picture is all over
the town. It's eighty years since Wilfred caught
that train; you still see SHREWSBURY on the white
illuminated name-plates, as he saw them.
Still there, the blood-red abbey. And still here,
the swollen Severn. Timbered houses pulled down
and towers put up, but still, he'd know this place.

I close my eyes. I call him back. His words
from a discarded manuscript – *What though
we sink from men as pitchers falling, many
shall raise us up.* I see him, in a crowd
of boys and girls, streaming out of the Technical School
- now swept away – that stood on the English bank;
sixteen, a smooth-cheeked student, carrying
his poetry textbooks under one arm, walking
across this river.

        When the floods recede
they'll leave a legacy of dirt, soaked deep
into the fabric. Rubbish, fallen leaves
and cardboard cartons, human waste, floats down,
choking the wells, as he wrote home from France.
This ancient bridge rebuilt and widened, using
the same stones, Wilfred's generation gone -
or carrying wounds round with them, which don't bleed.
Water, from Wales and England, hurrying past
the bursting arches, tidemarks long submerged,
so we can't see them, as we cross the stream.
The rubbish forming floating islands, which
the current pushes, finds its own way through.

POSTSCRIPT

TED HUGHES

A Picture of Otto

You stand there at the blackboard: Lutheran
Minister manqué. Your idea
Of Heaven and Earth and Hell radically
Modified by the honey-bee's commune.

A big shock for so much of your Prussian backbone
As can be conjured into poetry
To find yourself so tangled with me -
Rising from your coffin, a big shock

To meet me face to face in the dark adit
Where I have come looking for your daughter.
You had assumed this tunnel your family vault.
I never dreamed, however occult our guilt,

Your ghost inseparable from my shadow
As long as your daughter's words can stir a candle.
She could hardly tell us apart in the end.
Your portrait, here, could be my son's portrait.

I understand – you never could have released her.
I was a whole myth too late to replace you.
This underworld, my friend, is her heart's home.
Inseparable, here we must remain,

Everything forgiven and in common -
Not that I see her behind you, where I face you,
But like Owen, after his dark poem,
Under the battle, in the catacomb,

Sleeping with his German as if alone.